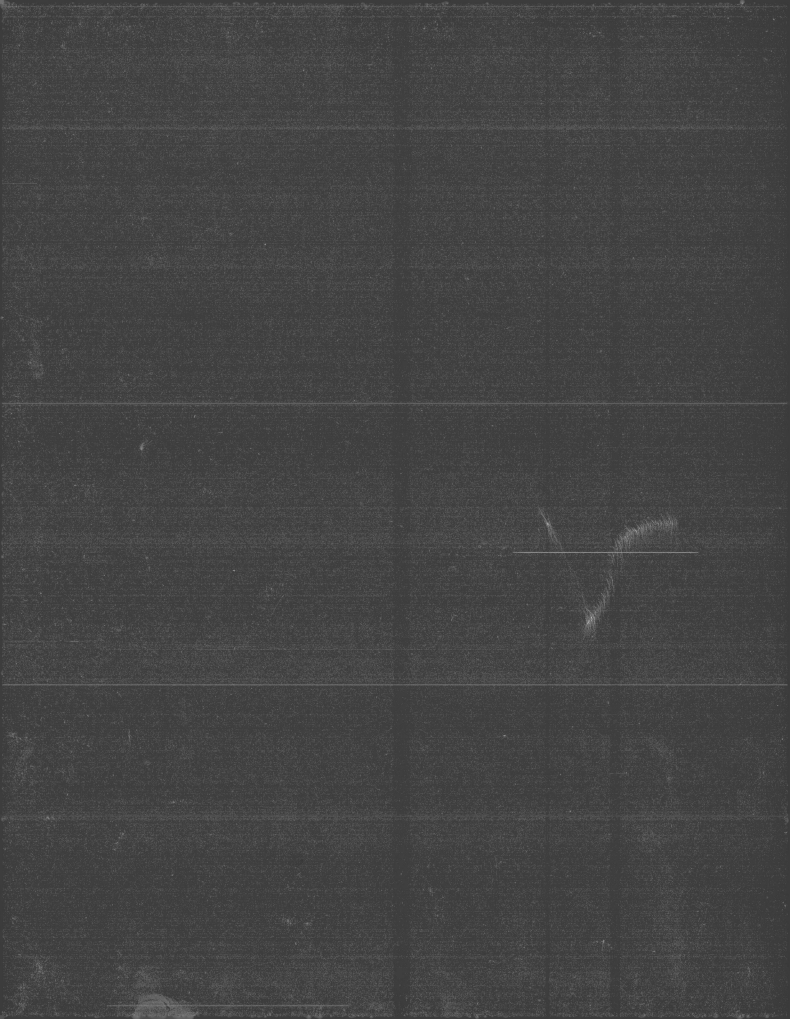

1001
Things to Spot
Long Ago

Gillian Doherty

Illustrated by Teri Gower

Designed by Susannah Owen

Edited by Felicity Brooks
Series designer: Mary Cartwright
History consultant: Dr Anne Millard

Contents

Things to spot

The pictures in this book show different scenes from long ago. On every page there are lots of things for you to find and count.

There are 1001 things to spot altogether. The example pages below show what you need to do to find them all.

This tells you when and where the scene took place.

Each little picture shows you what to look for in the big picture.

The grey number shows how many of that thing you need to find.

A castle feast
England, 600 years ago

2 roasted peacocks   3 trumpets   1 juggler   8 jugs   7 pies   10 knives   2 lutes   10 silver goblets   5 fish   6 money pouches

14   15

There are all kinds of other things to spot scattered throughout the book. They are gathered together in the museum at the end of the book.

You can find out what you need to do to find them on pages 30 and 31.

There's a spider like this one hidden in each big picture. Can you find them all?

3

At the market
Mesopotamia, 4000 years ago

9 donkeys

7 baskets of grapes

9 clay bowls

1 runaway wheel

10 necklaces

9 baskets of dates

10 sacks of grain

8 palm trees

6 baskets of apricots

10 copper bowls

Pharaoh's court
Egypt, 3500 years ago

10 beaded collars

9 white fans

2 pairs of red sandals

3 stools

10 wine jars

4 monkeys   1 harp   3 patterned rugs   10 bracelets   2 chests

Watching a play
Greece, 2300 years ago

1 mask with a beard

9 red cushions

1 crane

10 people laughing

8 people
eating

1 man
sleeping

8 hats

1 lyre

4 green
tunics

1 altar

In the garden

Rome, 2000 years ago

1 fountain

2 wooden dolls

1 abacus

8 statues

10 fish

10 red roses   3 scrolls   9 birds   2 slaves sweeping   10 apples

A Viking voyage
Norway, 1200 years ago

10 seagulls

9 chests

5 red cloaks

2 wagons

8 headscarves

10 plain shields   6 sheep   10 barrels   8 axes   9 chickens

A castle feast
England, 600 years ago

2 roasted peacocks   **3** trumpets   **1** juggler   **8** jugs   **7** pies

10 knives 2 lutes 10 silver goblets 5 fish 6 money pouches

The artists' workshop
Italy, 550 years ago

8 paint palettes

7 mallets

8 sketches

9 writing quills

10 paintbrushes

6 dirty shirts 7 easels 1 portrait of a lady 5 pots of red paint 6 black rats

An Inca farm
Peru, 500 years ago

9 hoes

8 babies in slings

5 people scaring birds

10 baskets of corn

9 women weaving

7 boats

9 sacks of potatoes

3 rope bridges

10 llamas

9 bundles of wood

Going hunting

India, 350 years ago

3 rifles

10 swords

5 white horses

2 elephants

8 blue turbans

3 tigers

10 gold tassels

9 arrows

6 hunting dogs

9 white feathers

Dressing up
France, 250 years ago

7 decorated boxes   **5** hairbrushes   **9** blue feathers   **8** fans   **4** hand mirrors

1 bird in a cage   6 pink ribbons   3 cats   2 parasols   10 yellow bows

A wagon train
North America, 200 years ago

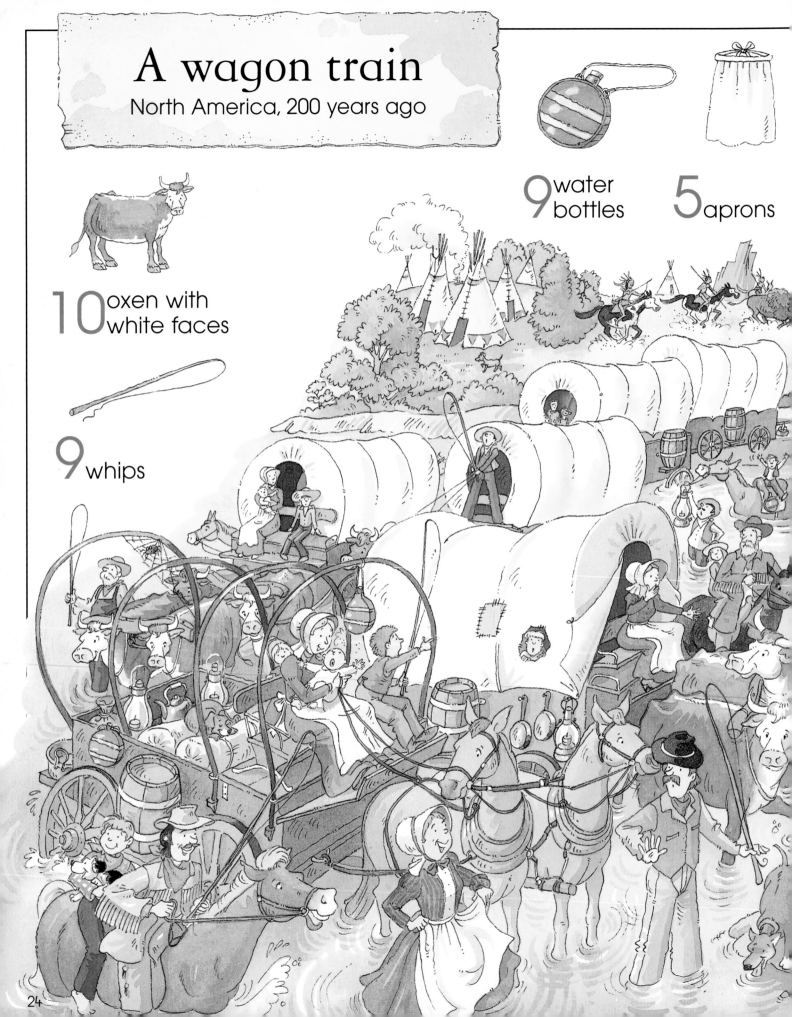

9 water bottles

5 aprons

10 oxen with white faces

9 whips

 **10** barrels    **8** buffaloes    **10** wagons    **7** black and white horses    **5** lanterns

6 teepees

25

Going shopping
England, 130 years ago

4 bells

7 dolls

3 rolls of red cloth

1 monkey

10 pigeons

5 baskets of flowers

1 rocking horse

4 lampposts

9 jars of sweets   8 shawls

The drive-in movies

North America, 45 years ago

8 ketchup containers

9 drinks with straws

10 slices of pizza

9 boxes of popcorn

10 hot dogs

2 pink cars

1 movie screen

4 snack carts

7 cheerleaders

10 speaker posts

At the museum

Museums help you to find out about people and things from long ago. This museum contains things from this book. Can you find which scene each thing is from? The answers are on page 32.

7 top hats

9 helmets

7 blue trays

8 toy hoops

3 cups and saucers

10 newspapers

6 black umbrellas

9 chisels

7 leather books

7 perfume bottles

6 cauldrons

3 cradles

7 red pompoms

10 silver spoons

8 flower pots

1 tailor's dummy

9 drinking horns

2 gold goblets

9 gold coins

9 blue cushions

8 keys

7 white pompoms

5 brooms

Answers

Did you find all the things from the museum on pages 30 and 31? Here's where they all were:

8 toy hoops:
Going shopping
(pages 26 and 27)

6 black umbrellas:
Going shopping
(pages 26 and 27)

7 top hats:
Going shopping
(pages 26 and 27)

9 helmets:
A Viking voyage
(pages 12 and 13)

7 blue trays:
The drive-in movies
(pages 28 and 29)

3 cups and saucers:
Dressing up
(pages 22 and 23)

10 newspapers:
Going shopping
(pages 26 and 27)

9 chisels:
The artists' workshop
(pages 16 and 17)

7 leather books:
Dressing up
(pages 22 and 23)

7 perfume bottles:
Dressing up
(pages 22 and 23)

6 cauldrons:
A Viking voyage
(pages 12 and 13)

3 cradles:
An Inca farm
(pages 18 and 19)

7 red pompoms:
The drive-in movies
(pages 28 and 29)

10 silver spoons:
A castle feast
(pages 14 and 15)

8 flower pots:
Going shopping
(pages 26 and 27)

9 drinking horns:
A Viking voyage
(pages 12 and 13)

2 gold goblets:
A castle feast
(pages 14 and 15)

9 gold coins:
A castle feast
(pages 14 and 15)

9 blue cushions:
Watching a play
(pages 8 and 9)

8 keys:
A castle feast
(pages 14 and 15)

7 white pompoms:
The drive-in movies
(pages 28 and 29)

1 tailor's dummy:
Going shopping
(pages 26 and 27)

5 brooms:
In the garden
(pages 10 and 11)

With thanks to Don and Susan Sanders
for advice on *The Drive-in movies*

First published in 1999 by Usborne Publishing Ltd, Usborne House, 83-85 Saffron Hill, London EC1N 8RT, England. www.usborne.com